THE FIRST
FIVE
MINUTES

THE FIRST FIVE MINUTES

SCHOOL SHOOTING
SURVIVAL GUIDE
*for Administrators
and Teachers*

DANIEL DLUZNESKI

Former Emergency Management Coordinator
Pinellas County Public Schools, Florida
Lieutenant U.S. Secret Service RET.

Copyright ©2022, Daniel Dluzneski

All Rights Reserved. This book may not be reproduced in whole or in part without the written consent of the publisher, except by a reviewer who may quote brief passages in a review. Nor may any part of this book be reproduced, stored in a retrieval system, or transmitted in any form or by any means, electronic, mechanical, photocopying, recording, or other, without the written permission of the publisher.

ISBN: 979-8-88831-031-1 (Ebook)

ISBN: 979-8-88831-032-8 (Paperback)

Cover Design: AuthorSupport.com

Cover Imagery: Shutterstock/David Whitemyer

CONTENTS

Introduction | 1

Prevention Measures | 7

Preparation | 23

Unique Situations | 53

New Technologies | 63

Conclusion | 69

About the Author | 75

INTRODUCTION

An active shooter attack lasts only 3 to 5 minutes on average, according to the FBI.[1]

This guide will prepare administrators, teachers and parents to keep students and staff alive during those critical first minutes of a potentially catastrophic event. It also outlines practical, realistic and inexpensive methods to protect your building and classrooms that will delay and deter a shooter from entering your school.

As the sole Emergency Management Coordinator for Safety and Security for our county school system, I was responsible for the safety of 150 schools and over 100,000 students. Not only did I review and revise the school safety procedures, but I also visited every

---
1 Active Shooter Study: A Quick reference guide 2014. www.FBI.gov/file-repository/as-study-quick-reference-guide-updatede1.pdf

individual school to assess the safety and security of the campus. I supervised, observed and participated in hundreds of active shooter training scenarios, helping them to improve the quality of their drills.

In my visits, I found that some schools did very well while others failed miserably. However, with each visit we learned valuable lessons that helped administrators to revise their protocols. These drills were critical as they would show where improvement was needed. Honestly, most of the time failure was the result of human factors and behaviors rather than a lack of technology.

I wanted to write this book to provide a practical guide that is easy to read and understand—one that is written by someone who has personal experience in school emergency preparedness. The goal of this book is for the reader to gain the confidence that they know exactly what to do to stay alive and prevent the deaths of others in these critical moments.

In my experience, many school administrators, teachers, students and parents hold on to the hope that local law enforcement will be able to react quick enough to assist in a shooter situation. Articles and books about this topic often have focused on public health factors such as gun control, limitation of local law enforcement, school mental health support or identifying individuals that may be prone to violence. I want to be clear that I am not minimizing the importance of those factors. However, I saw a lack of written guidance on helping school staff and students better protect themselves if such an event occurred.

There is a focus on expensive devices, such as metal detectors and technologies like apps, that allow you to lock all doors, alert the police, and notify and communicate with all school personnel, parents and the media with the push of a central button. I was heavily involved with a company that was going to provide a wide range of this technology in our county. It all looked terrific on the surface; however, you still need humans to observe the cameras, push the button, and make the call and the announcement. It takes a lot of training and repetition to be able to react automatically when you are in a state of extreme distress. Although these tools can be valuable, technologies can be expensive, fail or be disabled. The focus should be on the human factor, which is the most essential.

In my 24 years with the United States Secret Service, I will admit that I was not a big fan of training. It was boring and it took away from my daily routine. However, the repetition required to establish mental memory was crucial to my ability to be prepared in an eventual emergency.

The Secret Service recognized the importance of mental memory: being able to react without thinking. The drills had to be repeated until the reactions became second nature. Even many years after I retired, if I now hear a gunshot or sense imminent danger, I am reaching for my gun that is no longer there. In a similar fashion, active shooter drills need to be run regularly to establish mental memory or habit.

When I was hired by the school system, I quickly came to realize the challenges of the bureaucracy. School curriculum was the #1 priority for teachers. I couldn't seem to get an hour to train teachers to prepare for an active shooter situation. I did what I could with the limited training time and had them visualize what they would do in various "what if" scenarios. Teachers have one of the toughest jobs.

As I discuss later, for most teachers the reaction was to say, "I did not sign up for this," referring to preparing for a shooter in their school. Unfortunately, in these uncertain times teachers must be prepared.

This guide is not about gun control, how to prevent an individual from shooting up a school or how to keep guns out of their hands. I will not discuss in detail the various types of security technologies available because the expense is too much for most school budgets and because the internet can go down and these technologies can be disabled. I also will not criticize police responses to the many shooting events that have occurred.

This guide is about the critical need for administrators to set aside adequate time for these drills: the proper way to run an active shooter drill, and how to hold an after-drill discussion to revise and improve the school protocols. I will cover the crucial need for student involvement, especially at the high school level. I will also discuss how to prepare for the most vulnerable times (arrival, dismissal, and lunch) as well as unique issues that every school will encounter—for example, noisy rooms and hearing-impaired students and staff. You will also be able to download a comprehensive simple-to-follow school safety plan.

Most importantly, what I would want for the reader to take away from this book is that the safety of our children, staff members and visitors will depend on how teachers and administrators act in an emergency. When I was working at the White House on 9/11, my reaction kicked in instinctively from my training. I believe teachers and administrators will feel confident enough to take action and to save lives with the right kind of repetitive training and drill frequency.

Finally, I want to share one of my favorite stories from my years at our county school. A principal at one of our elementary schools liked to "throw a monkey wrench" into his drills to see if his staff had paid attention to the school safety plan. Part of that plan states "after initiating a drill or during a real active shooter event, DO NOT listen to or obey any announcements" because the shooter could be holding someone hostage and trying to get anyone to come out and be easy targets.

During one of his drills, the principal walked into the outdoor courtyard and, with a megaphone, said... "Go back to class, the drill is over." Repeating the same instruction again. The resident teachers ignored it; however, two substitute teachers opened their classroom doors and went back to teaching. Some of the young children spoke up and told the substitute that it was a trick and not to listen to that announcement. I made sure to applaud those kids when I saw them. That was only one of many times that I was pleasantly surprised by the intelligence and insight of these elementary children.

PREVENTION MEASURES

In order to prevent an event like this from happening, measures should be taken to address physical aspects of the school. Most recent school shooters are either current or former students at the school that they target. They are familiar with the school layout and access points that make the school vulnerable. The following will demonstrate the basic steps that should be taken to maintain a welcome atmosphere while still providing safety and security for the staff and students.

Limiting Campus Access

If you are reading this as a parent, I would like to ask

for your help. This discussion is mostly for parents of young elementary students.

It can be very stressful to drop off your new kindergartner or young elementary student at school and walk away. Many parents insist on escorting their child into the school and to the classroom. I can understand that the first few days of school can be scary for children, especially at a new school. However, I would suggest that after the first few days, you should drop your child off at the entrance. There is no reason for the parent to accompany the child all the way to the classroom and this behavior can inadvertently put your own child at risk.

There are not enough school staff to monitor every parent that is roaming the school grounds. If there was a real emergency, the principal would have no idea of the identity and number of parents who were on the school grounds and where they were located. Unfortunately, there is a potential for cases of an angry, armed parent or stepparent gaining access to the school. In one instance, a husband showed up quite calm and asked to see his wife, who was a teacher. Instead of having the teacher respond to the front lobby, the husband was allowed in and shot the teacher and some students.

I had my greatest arguments with parents over this issue of walking with their child every day to the classroom. I tried to explain that the school could not monitor parents' whereabouts inside the school. I asked what would happen if one of these parents roaming the school had bad intentions and received blank stares. It is difficult for parents to conceptualize the possibility of this kind of threat. Although incidents like these are rare, we must prevent them.

At one of the many parent meetings I attended, I was finally frustrated enough to ask two parents in the front row if they knew each other. They said no, they had seen each other at school but did not know anything about each other. I then asked if they would be comfortable if the other parent was alone with their child. Did they know that this adult was not a danger to their child? The answer is obvious. It didn't take long to sink in that there could be danger from another person.

I was able to convince most parents to end this practice of walking their children to the classroom. It then became policy in our county that parents were allowed to walk the children to class for only the first three days of the school year. After that, they were to be dropped off at the entrance. If the child was still experiencing anxiety, the school staff was happy to accompany that child to their classroom.

Classroom Doors and Windows

I observed some safety issues with doors and windows during my time with my county school system. Some of the older schools had doors with small windows that had wire mesh incorporated inside the glass. This seemed like a good deterrent to prevent a shooter from breaking the glass to open the door. I was told that a student accidentally broke the glass and was injured by the mesh, so these were no longer used. Another issue was classrooms with large observation windows to give students an opportunity to observe the class from the hallway. These windows could provide a shooter the perfect opportunity to shoot out the window.

The solution is to eliminate large human-sized observation windows that can be used as an entrance by an assailant. There are porthole type windows that can allow someone to look inside the classroom but aren't large enough to gain access. A common suggestion is bullet-proof glass, but that is cost prohibitive for most schools. A very affordable solution is to use window tint film that makes it harder to break the glass to gain access to the room. This is a good solution for schools that can't afford to replace the large observation windows.

Newer doors called ND-95 can also provide better security. They can be locked from the inside and are very strong doors. They do have a small slit window, which is a fire department regulation allowing a person to see inside the classroom but are not big enough to get your hand through.

Wedges, Door Blocks and Floor Deadbolts

Many companies have come out with different types of door stops as an additional means to secure the door from someone breaking in. Although very innovative and simple to use, most state fire marshals do not allow these types of door stops to be utilized. The reasoning is that during a fire the steps to get out of the classroom and the building should be a one-step process (i.e., unlock the door and get out). With the door stops it would become a two-step process—remove the door stop, unlock classroom door, and then get out. If the classroom is filled with smoke, it might be difficult to search for the door stop and then unlock the door.

We need an innovation that would allow the door to be easily barricaded while being able to escape fast if needed.

The practice of using door stops to prop open not only classroom doors but also outer doors during school time must stop. I have seen, more times than I can count, multiple outer doors propped open with rocks, wedges or books to assist someone who is running late or just too lazy to go through the front office. It is a perfect situation for a shooter who observes this type of behavior. Most shooters have attended or are students at the schools they target.

CAMERAS

I attended a conference that included architects, maintenance/plant operators and security personnel when I was working for the county school system. I had assumed the breakout sessions would address how to keep staff and students safe. I was disappointed that the main focus of these meetings was social justice. There is certainly a place for that important issue; but in this context, we should have discussed the urgent need to protect schools, as shootings were on the rise. As an analogy, if a person is dying, you need to provide urgent, lifesaving CPR. It isn't the time to address long-term prevention of what caused the illness.

I met the director of school security for the Oakland, California, school system at that conference. He talked about the struggle of securing his schools. He gave me a quizzical look when I asked about his camera system. He explained that he was still working on getting locks for his doors! Every school system has budgetary constraints. However, schools can make their buildings secure without expensive equipment.

School administrators usually install camera systems to catch bad behavior, at least in middle and high schools. Cameras provide a view of hidden stairwells, areas outside of bathrooms and outdoor entrances. However, it never takes long before the kids know where the cameras are. They figure out the best locations for mischief unseen.

As of the writing of this book, I am not aware of any studies done on the effectiveness of utilizing cameras to follow or deter an active shooter. I would imagine that a shooter could care less about cameras. He is not robbing a bank. His mission is to kill as many as possible and then die by suicide or by police action. A shooter might actually like the idea of his work being caught on camera. Furthermore, I have not seen any reports of school personnel looking at cameras and advising their staff of the location of a shooter. Cameras are likely not a deterrent for an active shooter. They can be a good source for locating a fire, a suspicious package, a hostage situation or a fight in a classroom. Later in this book, I will go over the pros and cons of various technologies that are available.

In-School Communication

Intercoms, PA systems and walkie-talkies are all great communicators to get announcements out quickly to as many people as possible. However, I cannot count the number of times that these systems failed during our drills. In some cases, only half the school classrooms could hear the announcements. The PA system at a few of our older elementary schools did not work through phones but rather an outdated microphone system, which often failed to work in all classrooms. I fought for years to establish announcements transmitting through the telephone system but ran into frustrating administrative barriers such as software/phone company incompatibility and budget issues. Unfortunately, it came down to a scary situation for principals who did not trust they could get the message out during an emergency.

Many principals turned to walkie-talkies, scrambling for solutions to keep their staff and students safe. Walkie-talkies have many issues. They are expensive, must be charged regularly, are sometimes unreliable and are subject to human error due to multiple radio channels. Many schools could only afford a limited number of walkie-talkies because of their high cost. This became an issue during an emergency because the staff with radios had to traverse the campus to warn others, putting themselves at risk.

During drills, walkie-talkies did serve a useful purpose: to communicate completion of lockdown drill and reporting issues, especially on our large high school campuses. During a real event, however, their efficacy may be negated by the potential chaos of voices talking over one another, screams and gunshots. We have had success utilizing cellphone texting between staff, principals and administrators, and email communication may also be an option.

However, I would caution that the light from a laptop in a darkened room might attract an assailant.

During a real emergency, schools have to use whatever means of getting the message out that they can, even if it requires putting a staff member in danger with face-to-face communication. This would only happen if every other part of the communication process breaks down, such as failure of power, internet service, or other internal communication systems. There must be a back-up plan!

Key Safety Personnel

The principal and the head plant operator (HPO) are the two most important people during a safety crisis, although every staff member has a role in the safety of the school. Administratively, the principal oversees the entire school. However, the HPO knows the school inside and out, and their role cannot be minimized. He (or she) traverses the entire school daily and may notice things of which the principal is not aware. The principal must work very closely with the HPO on a daily basis. The HPO maintains keys to all doors and knows every detail of the school grounds including gas, water, electric shut offs and fire alarms.

One issue that I noticed is that some principals don't respect or listen to the HPO and may not even include them in safety planning. The HPO should also act as liaison between the school and local police. The best scenario is to have the police involved in every drill at every school. If that is not possible, at least have the officers who would be responding familiarize themselves with the school layout and key safety personnel.

Make sure the police have the contact to obtain keys, maps and access points. More than likely that is going to be the HPO or principal. If either one of them is incapacitated, who is the next available to help? It is vitally important that these two key personnel work together to ensure the safety of the students and staff.

STUDENT INVOLVEMENT

A very important aspect of school safety that has waned over the years is student involvement. There were student safety groups or safety councils in high schools years ago. Students who aspired to be in the military, police or fire recruits would volunteer to traverse the campus, looking for issues that could cause injury such as broken doors, windows, trash, interior locker maintenance, etc.

I would like to see students take ownership of keeping their schools safe from a shooter as school shootings have become more common.

Of the 17 county high schools that I visited frequently, I could gain access to every one of them with

Prevention Measures

ease. In some that I tested, I could walk the campus with no one challenging me for up to an hour. Although this did not happen in the elementary and middle schools, most high schools are so large and spread out that it is difficult to be completely sealed off from outsiders.

Every school should have only one entrance after the arrival period is over. All the other entrances should be locked as soon as school begins. It was not uncommon for me to find doors being propped open with rocks, wedges, books or whatever object was handy. As most school shooters are either current or past students at the school they target, they are usually watching and know which doors are propped open or unlocked.

Student involvement can be as simple as traversing the school, looking for areas that an assailant can enter such as the propped door or window or the unlocked gate for deliveries from so called trusted services. Some schools have exit gates with push bars on the inside that can easily opened by slinging a backpack over the gate into the push bar.

Administrators should encourage students to get involved, troubleshooting safety measures. We should bring back the idea of a school safety council, not only to promote students to speak up if they hear of a threat but also to help keep the physical outlay of the school secure. I have seen videos of a shooter who just casually walked into the school. A mass shooting could be prevented by simply thwarting the shooters' attempt to enter, rather than giving them free access to the school grounds.

OUTER PERIMETER

A school should look inviting; however, for the safety of staff and students there must be fencing that surrounds the school. Some of my district schools were within 20-30 feet of major roadways, and children running out into traffic was a real concern. So, this fencing measure does two things: prevents students from leaving and others from entering. Fencing should be a minimum of 6 foot tall, but an 8 foot fence is even better.

Outer gates at large schools work well to control vehicle traffic or to close off traffic once school begins. There should be adequate lighting at night, especially in the parking lots. Cameras positioned for views of the parking lots and entrances should be able to swivel or rotate to the movement of individuals. Shrubbery and bushes need to be trimmed low enough so as not to provide cover for intruders or burglars. Inner office staff should have a clear line of sight for anyone walking up to the main entrance of the school.

The front roadway of the school should have a lane for emergency vehicles only and restricted use of this lane should be enforced. This was always an issue with students and parents using the lane for parking and to wait for students at dismissal.

Once the school day begins, the outer gates should be closed, and the outer school doors should be locked with **only one entrance** used for all visitors. Some schools have used cameras at the entrance along with a speaker so that the visitor can identify themselves. In reality, unless the person is seen carrying a weapon, the staff is going to let everyone in. In my opinion, this is a waste of money. If someone with bad intentions wanted to get into the front entrance, they could just wait for somebody to open the door or grab a staff person who can enter with a key card. The only answer is that front lobby staff remain vigilant and observant of all visitors.

Inner Perimeter

Once someone is allowed into the main entrance of the school, there should be a front office lobby area where every visitor must show identification and sign-in before entering the school. The lobby area is one of the schools' most vulnerable areas and must be addressed to implement the security process.

Many school lobbies have open counters which could be jumped over or half doors which swing open, allowing easy access to the interior of the school. I succeeded in closing off and securing these lobby areas in 75% of our schools with glass partitions to prevent easy entry beyond the lobby.

At first, the glass partition appearance turns people off, because it looks and feels too secure, almost claustrophobic. However, parents understand after it is explained that the staff must be kept safe in order for their children to be safe. We have had incidents of angry parents jumping over counter tops, gaining access to every area inside the school. The partition must be tall enough so it is not easy to climb over and low enough at the bottom so that someone can't grab the staff or reach the inner door buzzer to gain access. The partition does not have to be bullet proof but must be thick enough to avoid someone smashing it with a fist or other object.

Every school in the country has a different method of identifying and checking the background of visitors to determine whether they should be allowed into the school. Frequent visitors should be checked at least once a week, and infrequent visitors checked every time they visit. Each person attempting to access the school needs to show photo identification. The school should use a contract service so that front lobby staff can check the criminal background of the individual. The staffer will then buzz the individual into the school.

Even with the increase in school shootings, the issue of who belongs or is authorized to be in the school is a matter of complacency. I could roam any school unabated with no pass required, from elementary up to high school, before every school in my district had an armed school resource officer (SRO). As long as I looked like I knew where I was going with a purpose, everyone was friendly and welcoming. All the teachers waved hello, students would greet me with a smile, and maintenance workers would nod in my direction.

In my mind, I kept thinking that an assailant would receive the same greeting then proceed to hurt these welcoming students and staff. It is difficult, even in this day and age, not to be complacent. It is so much easier to just say hello and not challenge someone who doesn't have a pass. No one likes confrontation, especially with a stranger.

However, now more than ever, it must be done. Politely ask if you can help the person. Say "I see you are not wearing a pass. Can I direct you to the front office?" Or better yet, escort them to the front office to obtain a pass. Let your inner radar go to work. If the person is avoiding any direct contact by not looking at you or walking the other way, then notify the principal or the SRO, if your school has one. Teachers must question individuals without a pass and, most important, everyone who is required to have a pass must wear it. Even parents who are on campus daily and known to the students and teachers should be required to wear one. It has to be the same across the board, and not waived for the privileged some or the special parent who is the head of the PTA. Everyone wears the visitor's pass.

Classroom doors should stay locked the entire school day. If a teacher leaves an empty classroom, make sure it is locked behind them. Cafeteria doors can be locked; however, I found that there are few places to hide in an empty cafeteria. In most cases with the cafeteria empty it does not have to be locked. Try and have one system for announcements you can count on, whether it is through the phone system, PA or old-fashioned bullhorn. Make sure the system is tested daily, and keep your walkie-talkies fully charged.

PREPARATION

Preparing for an active shooter event at your school is a difficult, time-consuming, all-encompassing process. The best method to prepare for this type of event is through the right type of training and drills which you run with your staff. I believe that you prepare for the worst, so you are ready and confident when something happens, and you automatically know what to do. The following are the basic steps you will need to have that confidence.

When I started my employment with the county school system, I had no idea that I was going to be a one-man office. I found out that I alone would be supervising the safety plans and procedures for the 7th largest school district in the state of Florida, with 150 schools and more than 100,000 students.

As the only Emergency Management Coordinator,

I needed to assure all schools completed the required drills and to compile statistics and data as required by the state of Florida. My goal was to run active shooter drills that were as real as possible during the school day—a feat I mostly accomplished.

I personally attended PTA, SAC (School Advisory Council) and monthly teacher safety briefings. I produced and presented training sessions for principals and administrators to standardize the county drills and procedures. In addition, certain schools were designated by the county as hurricane shelters. I had the tedious task of assigning school personnel to man these shelters when we were under a hurricane threat. You can imagine the logistics of trying to keep teachers and administrators as close to their school as humanly possible. The worst part was I had to do all the assigning manually.

I found out quickly what I was up against when I tried to schedule active shooter drills at any of our schools. The county and the state had an academic grading system, and for the schools with lower grades, taking time away from the learning curriculum was extremely difficult. The state required active shooter drills to be completed quarterly, but my repeated recommendation that monthly drills would be more effective fell on deaf ears.

Prior to my arrival on the job, the following description is how a typical active shooter drill took place:

Teachers would be advised in advance of the date and time that the drill was to commence so they could prepare ahead of time to ensure the drill would take the least amount of time possible. For our teachers, there was so much pressure to complete curriculum that, understandably, ten precious minutes was too long to take away from their class time.

Before the drill even started, the teachers would cover the doors and windows, bringing children from outside, and forbidding anyone from going to the restrooms. The announcement would then come over the loudspeakers at the specified time with a chosen announcement such as "Code Red" or "Code Blue." The principal and other staff members with keys would spread out through the campus to make sure the teachers had properly locked their classroom doors. Then another announcement would be made that the drill was over, and classes could resume.

I witnessed this type of drill even though I had spread the word via email of the proper way to initiate a drill. I asked the principals what they would do if a real active shooter was on campus, and the majority simply replied that they would do the same thing they always did—spread out on campus to make sure the teachers had locked their doors.

When I tried to explain that this would likely result in them being shot and killed, I just got a blank stare. This was the same response from the elementary principals and administrators up through the high school level. They saw nothing wrong with traversing the campus during the drill because many of them believed that they could keep the children safe! I had to explain repeatedly that if they were dead, they would not be able to help anyone.

This was one of my biggest hurdles and I empathize with these principals. They couldn't imagine locking down in their offices and waiting for the police. They all felt that it was their responsibility to protect their kids. After many years, I finally was able to convince the principals to wait until the end of the drill then check that the classroom doors were properly locked before unlocking the doors.

One of the most creative active shooter drill codes was an elementary school announcement of "the pony will be delivered today." I can imagine that you could certainly get a child's attention with that code. However, if I'm a visiting county maintenance worker, a substitute teacher or a school volunteer, I wouldn't know what that announcement means. We have the same problem with any code that a school chooses that is unique to that particular school. A much better solution is a simple and easy to understand announcement such as "We are now in a lockdown."

I encouraged principals to give a long tone before the announcement and repeat it several times since many routine announcements that are heard often are inadvertently ignored.

This is the proper way to run an active shooter drill for all schools:

- An announcement will be made by the principal or other administrator. "We are now in a lockdown," then repeated again. Precede the announcement by a long tone.
- All staff must then follow the lockdown procedures:
  - Instruct students to go to their safe area in the classroom.
  - Lock doors, or if already locked, open the door and scan the hallway for any stray students or staff and wave them in.
  - Turn off lights, close the blinds, cover the doors and windows, and have students sit on the floor, or if more comfortable, at their desks with heads down.
  - Have your cellphone handy and on silent.
  - It is important that once the door is locked, it remains locked until an administrator or law enforcement officer unlocks the door.
  - Do not open the door for any reason, whether it's someone you know, says

they are law enforcement or is a student. Opening the door during a real event can be deadly.
- Account for all the students you have in the room. Report missing students to staff; if you pulled students in from the hallway, please include them in your notification. Send that information to the designated email address.
- Teachers alone in their classrooms should lock themselves in the room with lights off and blinds closed.
- Ignore all bells, alarms and announcements.
- Students that are out of their room on a pass need to go to the nearest open classroom or bathroom and lock themselves in a stall.
- Students that are out at P.E. will be directed to the closest interior building. If that building is compromised, then they will be directed to a designated secondary location off campus.
- Office staff will attempt to communicate with classrooms through email.

- Administrator duties:

  - Principal will designate who locks doors to the office and lobby area. They should also designate who calls 911; however, during

a real event, anyone can and should call 911 immediately.
- If the intercom does not operate or is compromised, use a radio and, as a last resort, use the person-to-person grapevine.
- Make sure you place a sign on the front entrance door that the drill is taking place. (This of course is not the case during a real event.)
- The principal or any of the staff should not check that doors are locked during a drill.
- Have a plan in place to unlock doors quickly when the lockdown is over. Assign ample staff and assign each to unlock doors in specific areas. As you unlock doors, tell the classroom to hold until they hear the announcement that the drill is over and to continue classroom activities.
- Lockdown drill debrief—it is important to get feedback (good or bad) and document discussion in the safety meeting minutes.

Drill issues

Fire alarms–Social media can sometimes be the enemy of a safety coordinator. At one time, rumors were circulating through social media that a shooter or co-conspirator would pull the school fire alarm, giving the shooter a chance to pick off students and staff as they escaped outside. This scenario never actually took place. Logically, after the first or second shot, everyone would scatter, making it difficult for the shooter to target anyone. However, the rumor persisted and periodically, when the fire alarm was set off, students and staff were afraid to leave the classroom. Along with the Fire Marshal, we agreed that the teacher should step outside the classroom during the fire alarm and scan the hallway, listening for anything out of the ordinary, then proceed outside. It is important during a fire alarm that everyone, including staff and all teachers, exit the building.

Outside activities–For situations like outdoor P.E., procedures need to be tailored for both your school layout as well as the age group of the students. In an active shooter situation, it may not be best to go back into the school building, and for younger children (elementary age), it is important to keep them together. It might be best to choose a designated exterior room, stand-alone building or hidden area that that is close to the outside P.E. area. An alternative, especially in the case of high school age students, might be to have a designated church or business, close to the school, as a secondary location if students get caught outside during an active shooter event.

Substitute teachers–every new or regular substitute must have training for active shooter events.

This is just one reason that it is important to have a standardized system for all schools, so regardless of which grade or school they are assigned to, the substitute will respond the same as the regular staff.

Police & Fire Departments–If the school does not have a Special Resource Officer (SRO) assigned, then local law enforcement should be invited to attend the drills. In addition, local law enforcement should have a map of the school including classroom numbers, along with the location of electrical power, gas, alarms, etc. The fire department should have lockboxes in case a school fire breaks out after hours, and the police or a designated local police official should have access to that lockbox in order to get into the school during a lockdown.

It is important that the local police familiarize themselves with the school and have contact information for the Head Plant Operator and the Principal, in case of an emergency.

After action meetings–After the drill is over is the perfect time to discuss what may happen during a real event. I would recommend scheduling a short debrief meeting after each drill. These are some critical issues that need to be discussed and prepared for:

- Have a designated area after a real event for parents to come pick up their children. Keep in mind that parents will come no matter how many texts you send telling them to stay away.

- Have a designated media location.
- Have a designated command location.
- Text message parents as soon as possible. It is a horrific event, but the message must get out there. Make it clear and simple. "We are in a lockdown. There is an active shooter on campus."

DRILL FREQUENCY AND TYPE OF DRILLS

Ideally, I would like for active shooter drills to take place at a minimum of **once per month**. However, this is usually up to a state education board or the county school board. I would encourage parents to speak to your local representative to have active shooter drills performed more frequently. Repetition will invoke mental memory, which in turn will enable more confidence and a quicker, automatic reaction when an emergency happens.

Be forewarned that having more frequent drills can cause headaches. I was at an elementary school during an active shooter drill, acting as a "ghost" to observe how they were reacting and locking down. About halfway through the drill, I had a parent at the entrance gate screaming to get in so they could pick up their child for an appointment. Even after I explained what was occurring, the parent was angry and non-compliant. I told her she would just have to wait.

As a parent myself, I do understand. We did not put out an announcement to parents that the drill was going to occur. I disagree with telling children to go home and notify parents that there is going to be an active shooter drill at school tomorrow. Parents do give up control once the child is in the school as essentially it is the schools' responsibility to keep the children safe.

Pros and Cons of Unannounced Drills

The Pros:

An unannounced drill will show you more accurately how you will perform in a real-life event.

I had a colleague tell me about a real active shooter event that occurred at his wife's elementary school. She was the assistant principal.

Apparently, a young man in the neighborhood was upset with his mother's boyfriend. He began shooting not only at his mom's house but at the school next door with a semi-automatic rifle. He had no intention of entering the school, but rightly the school went into a lockdown. The assistant principal, who had been very proactive in drilling for this type of scenario, later told her husband that about a third of the teachers completely froze during the lockdown. They did nothing and absolutely panicked.

My point is that administrators need to see how people will react and unannounced drills provide the closest scenario to a real event. There will be mistakes—doors left unlocked, unmade phone calls, misplaced children and many others. However, mistakes are preferred during a drill than in the real event. Those issues can be easily fixed. Once a step is forgotten or a door is left unlocked, **they never forget it again!**

One elementary school principal was particularly memorable to me because she was always ready to do an unannounced drill and even encouraged it. She wanted to see how her staff and teachers would react. During drills on her campus, there were two incidents that provided good lessons.

One teacher forgot her keys that day, and this school had classroom doors that needed to be locked from the outside. Since she had no way of locking the door, she thought it would be a good idea to grab the inside handle, hold the door shut and hope for the best. It just so happened her classroom was one of the doors I tried to open during the drill. I felt resistance but did not force the door open, although I could have easily done so. Later, after the drill was over, I went back and talked to the teacher. She was in a panic and just held that door shut with all her might. I explained that she could have instead barricaded the door, as a shooter will most likely move on to the next door if it wasn't easily opened.

During another unannounced drill, an elementary student was allowed to go alone to the restroom, as the students just came back from the playground. Most schools require a buddy system for elementary students when using the restroom. In this case, his teacher allowed him to go alone. He unfortunately got caught out in the hallway during the drill. I explained to him to go back into the restroom and lock himself in one of the stalls. I then continued to traverse the campus, observing the drill. Three times the child came back out of the bathroom confused about where his classmates had gone. Later, the teacher was very upset that she had misplaced that student, out of a class of 25 kids who just came back from the playground. This was a lesson that she will never forget. As I have said previously, teachers have one of the hardest jobs in the world.

The bottom line is that unannounced drills show our glaring mistakes and help with fixing the issues before a real event occurs.

The Cons:

Unannounced drills sometimes prove embarrassing for principals when they are not performed well and critical mistakes are made. In addition, parents can get very upset by unannounced drills. However, parents do have the right to opt out of any of these active shooter drills, although I think that is a big mistake.

If you trust the school to teach your children, you should also trust them to keep your children safe. If a child comes home and says the school had an active shooter drill that day, the school and the school board will definitely receive some angry phone calls. Another problem is that any planned activity at the school is going to be delayed. If your school insists on utilizing only announced drills, discourage the staff to prepare in any way before the drill commences.

Lockdowns versus Options-Based Training

There are two philosophies regarding training for active shooter situations. First, "lockdowns" have been used for over 30 years, more commonly since the Columbine shooting. A newer approach is called "options-based training," which incorporates the business-world model of "Run, Hide, Fight." This ALICE method, which stands for Alert-Lockdown-Inform-Counter-Evacuate, is a federal Homeland Security Department program originally created for use in workplace settings. The purpose is to give the teacher the option of remaining in a lockdown or getting out of the school away from the attacker.

According to the National Association of School

Psychologists and the National Association of School Resource Officers, "...we believe that lockdown is an essential component, if not the foundation, of any such training and that the hierarchy of training and education offers effective options for how to provide training."[1]

Lockdowns work. The reason is a shooter only has a certain amount of time, 3-5 minutes on average, to target victims. It takes too much effort to breach a locked door when it is easier to find victims elsewhere. Lockdowns are simple and with drilling and training can become second nature. In fact, some schools now keep their classroom doors locked during school hours, which I highly recommend. Lockdowns keep teachers and students in one safe and secure location. And in a drill situation, after the drill is completed, students can continue their classwork.

With options-based drills, teachers have the option to "run" if possible, "hide" if running is not possible or to "fight" the assailant if the room is breached. It is my opinion and strong recommendation that options-based training should be reserved only for high school and possibly certain middle school teachers.

In my opinion, options-based training should never be made available for elementary teachers.

---
[1] "Best Practice Considerations for Armed Assailant Drills in Schools," www.Nasponline.org/resources-and-publications/resources-and-podcasts/school-safety-and-crisis/systems-level-prevention/best-pracrice-considerations-for-armed-assailant-drills-in-schools. Updated April 2020.

The First Five Minutes

Trying to "run" with small children can lead to terrible possibilities: seeing deceased victims, getting separated from their group, becoming a victim themselves, panicking and not being able to flee at all or becoming injured trying to exit the school.

According to NASP and NASRO, "it is important that options-based drills take into account the developmental levels of students as well as the physical layout of the school campus (e.g., ease of access to outside doors and proximity of places to hide other than classrooms)."[2]

The Parkland shooting at Marjorie Stoneman High School was unusual for two reasons. First, the fire alarm was set off and second, the shooter randomly ran from floor to floor looking for victims instead of concentrating on one location. The confusion for both teachers and students was a perfect chaotic scene for the shooter. Teachers were unsure about taking everyone out for the fire alarm. Fortunately, some of the teachers heard shots as they prepared to exit and hurried back to their classrooms and locked down. Some teachers tried to take their students and run, thinking that the shots they heard were in the opposite direction of where they were traveling. It proved a mistake. The shots were echoing, and they were taking their students towards the shooter.

---

2 "Best Practice Considerations for Armed Assailant Drills in Schools," www.Nasponline.org/resources-and-publications/resources-and-podcasts/school-safety-and-crisis/systems-level-prevention/best-practice-considerations-for-armed-assailant-drills-in-schools. Updated April 2020.

Preparation 39

Parkland is just one example of why I disagree with options-based training. The ALICE or Run, Hide, Fight protocols are geared for the adult business world. They were not created specifically for schools. In ALICE training, administrators and staff are to monitor cameras during a real event and broadcast to teachers where the shooter is traveling within the school so they can determine whether to run. I think this is a dangerous mistake to put a school administrator in the position of making critical decisions that could result in deaths of children and their school staff.

Another example for why the simple lockdown method is better is the case of a school with physically handicapped and/or mentally challenged children. You can imagine how hard it is for teachers to proceed as fast as they can to get disabled children into wheelchairs or mentally challenged children to follow instructions. It can also be difficult to keep these students quiet and orderly.

I can't stress enough the importance of keeping an active shooter protocol simple. In a real event, even adults may panic and can't remember what to do. For example, part of every drill is to have a designated front office person call 911 and tell the dispatcher the school is running a drill and that police do not have to respond. During one drill event, the individual forgot to make that call. They forgot drill! What if an individual forgot to call 911 event? The simpler a protocol is, the more likely the response can become automatic. When the real event happens, that 911 call will be made every time.

Lockdowns work if the human element is trained properly and follows the strict protocol of the steps needed to secure the classrooms and the school.

TRAINING FOR IMPLICIT MEMORY

Safe Havens International is a school safety and training institution, which has initiated training scenarios for different types of school emergency situations. What it found was surprising: many hours of standard training for certain situations did not provide the expected results.

For example, in one scenario a teacher and her class were outside at recess when an individual with a gun approached the group from the distance of about a football field. Most of the teachers with 3-1/2 hours of training incorrectly tried to approach the man and disarm him! The majority of the untrained teachers correctly took the children quickly inside to safety and called 911. This type of behavior was seen across multiple emergency scenarios, not just active shooters. Teachers with no training did better than the teachers with training.[3]

---

[3] "Put Training to the Test" by Michael Dorn, January 1, 2018 www.asisonline.org/security-management-magazine/articles/2018/01/put-training-to-the-test/.

Preparation

This brings up an interesting question: are we overtraining our school personnel? It certainly seems that way from these findings. In my training sessions, I try to invoke the concept of mental or implicit memory. This is a common approach with professional athletes, along with muscle memory. Mental memory is an action that is done without conscious thought.

Many years ago, there was a world class high jumper named Dwight Stones. Before every jump, he would **mentally** go through the actions and processes of his upcoming jump. You could see him nodding his head to each step of his jump. To some it looked odd or comical; however, it worked for him. Other examples of implicit memory include putting on a seat belt, riding a bike, driving a car or buttoning a shirt. In a similar fashion, I want teachers and staff to be able to react to an active shooter automatically without conscious thought.

When I was employed with the Secret Service, we were required to qualify with our service weapon once per month. We all had completed the same training program of how to shoot with the goal of developing mental and muscle memory. We practiced each step repeatedly—draw your weapon, lock out your arms, control your breathing, focus on the front sight, squeeze the trigger, fire the weapon. We did it again and again until it became rote, locking the entire process into our subconscious brain so we could react without thinking. We became more confident in the process with this implicit memory. When the time came to react in a real situation, stress, anxiety and emotions were less likely to interfere with the reaction.

I tried to instill that kind of memory and confidence in the school drills, practicing each step from the first announcement of lockdown to the teachers and staff completing their checklists and on to the end of the drill with unlocking the class doors. In my opinion, it is much easier to invoke implicit memory with the lockdown approach. Options-based training is not compatible with development of implicit memory. Every situation is different and requires the teacher to make critical decisions in a state of stress. Why would we require a teacher to decide in a split second what options they have when the easiest and safest thing to do in an active shooter event is lockdown? We know from studies that even with extensive training teachers do not perform well with options.

For those considering options-based training, consider the critical decisions steps and responsibilities of the teachers:

- First, the teacher must decide which is safer for themselves and their students—locking down or running.

- If the decision is to run, the teacher would have to convince every student to follow.
- They must decide when to run and where is the safest place to run.
- When running, the teacher and students may encounter any of the following: gunfire, screaming and pleas for help; dead or injured classmates and teachers; panic and pileups at exit doors; or students trampling each other in a rush to get out.

The best and most simple option and one that should be happening most of the time is locking down. Simple lockdown steps include locking the door (classrooms should already be locked which saves this step), turning off the lights, sitting quietly in an area of the room away from windows, silencing cell phones, barricading the door if the shooter is close then waiting for the police. Remember, most school shootings are completed within 3-5 minutes, even before the police have time to respond.

Drill Tools

A double-sided credit card sized quick reference guide for teachers and administrators can be a valuable tool to be used during a drill or real event. They could quickly check what they need to do, because in a real situation, no one knows exactly how they will react.

TEACHER BUY-IN

Teachers need to know and feel confident that the administration has their back. I just saw an article that the teacher shortage is at an all-time high in my state of Florida. Many factors have caused this, including the pandemic, school shootings, low pay, new laws passed and teacher burnout. I can only focus on the school shooting incidents and caution again that they are a rarity. However, they also occur outside of school, as I have seen in recent mall shootings.

I have attended many briefings with teachers and staff. Even weeks after a school shooting, the teachers are scared. Teachers are there to teach, nurture, encourage, inspire and challenge their students. I can name a handful of my own teachers that inspired and encouraged me. Even today I am good friends with my former algebra teacher, and I was horrible at math!

The teaching profession today is so different from decades ago. Not only have school shootings changed the culture, but the intense pressure to keep the school in good graces with the administration—meaning keeping the school as an 'A' school to ensure money from the state—makes teaching a very hard job. Now teachers also fear for their lives and the lives of their students.

I am here to say that teachers do not have to fear for their lives. They must be aware, confident, determined and above all calm during a crisis. As hard as that is to do, this attitude should carry over into their private lives, not just at school. I want teachers to be trained properly and to know immediately what to do in an emergency. There are plenty of books that will tell you what to do and what steps to take in an active shooter scenario. Every time there is a school shooting, these steps are discussed. Without the repetitive drills within each school, the appropriate action and the mental memory will not be developed.

Active shooter drills are a pain. They take much longer than fire drills and cut into teaching time; they are a necessary evil and you want them over as soon as possible, but they are important and save lives.

When I meet with teachers, I often get questions of "what if" scenarios or hypothetical events that may or may not happen. Most of the questions are about forgetting a step or the possibility of panicking. No one knows how they will react during an emergency unless they have experienced one in a prior situation.

I emphasize to teachers that during our active shooter drills the steps they need to take are very few. They are already in a locked classroom. Help is coming. If they are calm, their students will remain calm. If the shooter targets their classroom door, they need to be determined to barricade the door and do everything in their power to keep them out.

Parent Buy-In

Parents need to be assured that training and drills are essential to keep their child safe. If parents know that not only is the school drilling properly but that the local police are familiar with the school and its layout, it will go a long way to ensure parent buy-in on security measures that may at first seem overboard, but will provide safety for their children and staff.

Age Appropriate Drills

When I was in elementary school, the threat of a nuclear attack during the Cuban Missile Crisis was real. I do not recall being anxious or scared during the "Duck and Cover" drill that we ran during that time. We all just lined up in the hallway, squatted down, covered our heads and tried to be quiet. I remember it being hard after a while, because as kids we wanted to squirm and mess around. We also had fire drills back then where we had to stand up, get in a line and follow the teacher. Then we stood outside until it was time to go back in.

We didn't have to worry about many issues young

kids face today. However, the growing backlash against having small children participate in active shooter drills is concerning to me. If you want them to go to a particular school, then you must trust that the school administrators have a solid school safety plan.

If there is a concern about the safety plan, get involved and discuss your concerns at the PTA or school board meetings. Don't be afraid to ask to see the safety plan. Remember, school shootings are extremely rare. It is always better for the school administrators, teachers and students to be prepared for the occurrence.

The teachers often made it into a fun game when I performed active shooter drills at any of our elementary schools. The kids had to hide and be as quiet as possible. They would hide together inside an interior bathroom or a storage closet. Many times, the teacher would pick a child to be the leader of the drill.

I participated in many drills at more than 70 elementary schools and never once saw an anxious or fearful child. At the end of every drill, I would team up with the principal to start unlocking doors and see kids beaming and happy when we would praise the kids for accomplishing the important task.

While I traversed elementary schools during the drill, many times I would try to open the door and bang on the door and windows. Uniformly, I could not hear a sound coming from the classrooms. I felt very proud that during an active shooter drill, I would travel the entire campus and you would never know anyone was there. That was my ultimate goal for the drill.

It was important to me to concentrate on the elementary schools and work with their principals. We had a large number of these schools, many in isolated locations and more at risk. I also felt the smaller kids were more vulnerable and in need of greater protection. However, just because these kids were small does not mean they were naive.

The layout at one particular elementary school had clusters of satellite classrooms. From the outside you would go through a set of double doors into a vestibule of 4 classrooms in a semi-circle. To prepare for an active shooter drill, a designated teacher would have to first exit their classroom and lock the outer doors. The key to those doors was kept in the fire extinguisher cabinet.

Out of curiosity, I asked the teacher how they dealt with having a substitute teacher if there was a drill or an actual emergency. At least 2-3 kids jumped in and explained that they knew the location of the key and how to lock and unlock the outer doors. What a great idea! So, we had each of those children in that class take that key and make sure they could lock and unlock the outer doors. This would also be helpful if something happened to the teacher who was unable to get the outer doors locked.

As I stated at the very beginning, when the elementary school principal tried to trick his teachers into thinking the active shooter drill was over, the kids quickly realized it was a trick. Elementary kids are smart, perceptive and soak everything up. In many cases they may know what to do before the teacher!

Lockdown versus Lockout

There is one aspect of the active shooter drill and training that some find confusing—the difference between a lockdown and a lockout or "keep out."

A lockdown is used specifically if an intruder has entered school grounds. Any individual on school grounds who is carrying a weapon, acting in a threatening manner or taking violent action should call for a lockdown.

If an individual is cutting through the football field or walking their dog on school property that doesn't mean you go into a lockdown. I am not going to go through every hypothetical scenario. Obviously, there may be situations that require a judgement call.

A lockout, on the other hand, is used when there is police activity or a threat in the vicinity of the school such as a police chase, a domestic issue, a burglary or shots fired. Many individuals being chased by the police are not a direct threat to the school. They just want to get away from the police. They may seek to hide in a school or traverse the school. Obviously, you can go into a lockdown if this happens on school grounds.

A lockout consists of locking the main entrance door and outer or exterior doors which, as mentioned earlier in the book, should already be locked. All outside activities are cancelled; however, teaching can continue. Students should be escorted when traveling between classes through any outside courtyard or across open spaces on campus. Most importantly, the principal or assistant principal should be in contact with the police. An announcement that the school is back to normal can be made at the end of the lockout.

I received multiple phone calls from principals confused about whether to go into lockdown or lockout when they had police activity in their area. Often, they listened to inappropriate police direction and went into lockdown.

When the school went into a lockdown in that scenario, they sometimes were not advised that the police situation was over. They would have kids in the dark, for hours sitting on the floor quietly and waiting for someone to come and unlock the door.

Principals would call me to complain about the situation, asking if I could find out if the police situation was resolved. I advised them that if they were going to listen to the police and lockdown, a police officer should stay in communication or be present at the school until the event is over. If this wasn't feasible, it made more sense to lockout, remain vigilant, continue indoor class activities and stay in contact with the police.

UNIQUE SITUATIONS

Some of the aspects of school safety do not fall into specific categories. The following are just a few examples of situations that have come up in my experience during the many drills I have observed.

Most Vulnerable Times for an Active Shooter Event

An active shooter may take advantage of the most vulnerable times, which are **arrival, lunchtime and dismissal.** School assemblies also present vulnerability but are not as consistent as these school transition periods which occur at the same time each day.

One event that I will never forget was an incident

at a middle school located adjacent to a high school campus. The high school went into a lockdown, causing the middle school to follow suit. The middle school principal was greeting children as they arrived. On being notified of the high school lockdown, she noticed some of her students were coming from a 7-Eleven store less than a block away. Per protocol, she was supposed to immediately go into the school and lockdown.

She had to make several difficult and split-second decisions. Did she pull the students into the school or have the parents drive away with their students? Should she put herself in danger to alert those students coming from the 7-Eleven? She chose to get as many kids as possible into her school and lockdown but suffered post-traumatic symptoms of abandoning those kids coming from the 7-Eleven. Fortunately, it turned out to be a false report of a gun on the high school campus. Days later, I talked to the middle school principal and the incident was still on her mind. She thought those children at the 7-Eleven could have been shot or killed because of her decision.

It was these types of questions that came up during our drills—what to do and how to make a split-second decision in these types of circumstances. Principals and teachers care greatly about their students. In many ways, they consider the students as their own children.

The principal was distraught for a number of days, concerned about whether she made the right decision. I told her that there was no "right" decision. However, the **most important** decision was keeping herself safe. She could help no one if she was shot and injured or worse, dead.

There will be times that you have to make a critical decision. It is imperative that teachers and principals keep themselves safe first so they can help others.

Hearing Impaired Teachers and Students

It was our school district policy that every hearing-impaired student was assigned a hearing student who would warn them in the event of an emergency. In all the years of monitoring drills, I never observed a hearing-impaired student not being alerted. However, there was an instance of failure to alert a hearing-impaired teacher. This occurred because, on the day of the drill, that teacher's designated helper was sick, and the substitute teacher was not advised of their role. Going forward, the school assigned a back-up teacher in the event the primary helper was not there. This is just one example of the importance of drills to identify holes in the process and correct them before an actual event occurs.

Band Rooms, Cafeterias and Gymnasiums

At the same conference I mentioned above, I really wanted an answer to the dilemma of how to alert students and staff of a lockdown or active shooter situation who were in a noisy band room, gymnasium or cafeteria. Nobody had any ideas and most attendees had never thought about it. I asked band leaders and cafeteria assistants about this issue. The band leaders said that because of the noise level someone would have to physically step into the room and be recognized to alert the room that they were in a lockdown. The cafeteria personnel said the students were so loud during lunch that they could not hear their phone or feel a phone vibration, so they would have no idea if the school went into lockdown.

In our school system, children are allowed 30-45 minutes to have lunch and that time is not to be used for any other means. It was difficult for me to get a lockdown drill to happen during lunch time, even though that scenario must be practiced in a drill. The Columbine shooter used the lunch hour to take advantage of this vulnerable time to kill 13 and wound 20 students and staff.

I finally got approval for one of our high schools to run an announced drill during lunch. The school staff and I designated the staffers to separate the children by zones. Each staffer was designated a particular location around the cafeteria and outside tables to instruct students to run to a specific location. Most students complied. However, it would be chaotic in a real situation, but that isn't necessarily a bad thing. Chaos and students running in all different directions make it harder for a shooter to pick off targets. Remember, shooters want easy stationary targets because their goal is usually to kill as many people as possible.

In noisy rooms, I partnered with our county school fire marshal to come up with a solution, the best idea being to use a light system. We thought it was important to have the same alarms and codes for all rooms, since having different sounding alarms could cause confusion. We felt that consistency was a priority with 140+ schools in our county. We settled on a light system that activated once a lockdown was announced. We set up panels that hung on the wall in clear view for everyone in the room.

Ultimately, after much trial and error, we were unable to find a way to activate this light system for only the lockdown alert and from a central location. We need to invent a technology to alert students when noise prevents them from hearing a lockdown announcement.

Social Media

Most children these days have cell phones. Fortunately, they are put away during class time.

The First Five Minutes

:, in an emergency the phones come out of backpacks and messages start being sent. This is not necessarily a bad thing, as kids can communicate with parents, police and teachers.

But it becomes a problem when the rumor mill starts. I responded to a bomb threat at one of our largest 1,000 student high schools, which also was adjacent to a middle school with over 800 students.

As the students were being evacuated, the texts and posts started coming through Facebook and Twitter. Some of the messages were completely false. There were rumors of seeing a backpack with wires sticking out of it, of seeing someone place the backpack at a certain location and rumors of what sounded like an explosion.

These texts and posts caused more uncertainty for the first responders, administrators and parents, which led to parents rushing down to the school. Can you imagine thousands of parents coming to both schools to pick up their children? One of the fortunate actions we took was to have a large firetruck block the road leading to the schools. Once the school was cleared (the bomb threat was a hoax), then we allowed parents to meet their children at a designated area.

That was not the first time this happened. At another high school, the bomb threat was early in the day and cleared rather quickly. However, parents still wanted to pick up their children. The principal tried to assure the parents that the threat no longer remained, but to no avail. I mention this because as administrators you must be prepared for this kind of response, no matter the type of incident.

As we have seen in many of the shootings at schools, **parents are coming!** It doesn't matter what message the school puts out—false alarm, everyone is ok, there is no need to pick up your children—they are coming. I'm not going to lay blame, because as a parent, I would do the same thing.

My point about cell phones and texting is to be aware that false alarms and rumors are going to happen. However, the same technology can result in the reporting of helpful information like the location of the shooter, the child's location, injuries, etc. During a real event, we would have to trust that the students are passing along some factual information.

Bomb Threats

Bomb threats seem to happen a lot on high school campuses, curiously more often around test time. For school principals, the action to take in the event of a bomb threat is a judgement call. Each school office should have a standard bomb threat caller checklist and procedure.

During my time with the Secret Service at the White House, bomb threats occurred weekly at a minimum, sometimes more often. We had a lot of eyes on the White House grounds, and unless the bomb caller reported a specific area and description of the bomb package, we took it as a threat only. We would have our officers check the entire area, inner posts and outer perimeter, looking for any suspicious packages.

At one high school in my school district, a bomb threat was called in at least once per month. Every time this happened, the entire 800-person school would evacuate across the street and wait up to two hours for the school to be cleared. I would argue, but not insist, that evacuation was not required. Did the caller mention any specifics such as location in the school, classroom number, a teacher's name? Did they mention the time it would go off? Did they mention what the bomb looked like? Without these specifics, I would recommend that teachers and students search their respective areas, and if nothing was found, go back to normal operations.

If a suspicious item is found, by all means, evacuate the school. Ultimately, it is the principal's decision. They may choose evacuation as the first option to err on the side of caution. Everyone in the school should evacuate outside the school at a minimum distance of 1000 feet. The school evacuation plan should also have a secondary location, in the event that it takes a significant amount of time to assess the situation and clear the school. Some secondary locations may be locked during the day and may allow the school administration to have an access key.

Depending on the climate, the location should provide cover, bathroom facilities, heat and/or air conditioning and water. As mentioned earlier, because of social media and cellphones, parents are coming. So have your "Go Box" with a roster of students and a list of who is allowed to pick up the child. Ask for identification and have a staffer escort that child to the pickup point. You don't want panicked parents wandering around your school or your secondary location.

Fires & Bombs

I hesitate to add this section, but fear that in the future using fire or bombs may become a more common way for troubled individuals to attempt to increase victim counts. In past school incidents, there were individuals who thought it would create more havoc to start fires in the school before they started shooting.

Starting a fire serves the assailant no advantage to killing more victims. It just creates a lot of smoke, confusion and a distraction. Most shooters want easy access and the ability to roam freely inside the school to find multiple victims in confined area. Modern schools have adequate fire safety measures including sprinkler systems, fire retardant walls, fire resistant doors and two exit points from classrooms.

Bringing a bomb to school in a backpack could possibly hurt or kill a lot of people; however, the logistics are complicated. The backpack would have to be placed in crowded areas such as cafeterias, gymnasiums or assembly halls. In addition, the bomber would have to obtain a remote timing device or have it set off via cellphone. I believe the assailants want to see the results of their actions. This approach wouldn't work for that purpose. They may kill more people with their bomb, but they will never see the damage.

NEWER TECHNOLOGIES

Fortunately, we are on the cusp of some great technology to keep our schools safe. There are companies that monitor everything within a school and can lockdown the school with the touch of a button, monitor your school with motion detection camera systems and alert the police and fire departments. This technology is very expensive and is cost prohibitive for most public schools that don't even have door locks.

Metal Detectors

I don't agree with having metal detectors in schools. It is a panacea and serves only the purpose of convincing some individuals that the school is "doing something." During my time with the Secret Service, we used metal detectors at every Presidential venue. We had officers that were trained in the technical aspects of the detector-calibrating and evaluating the machine for use in proper detection. They may be unreliable if they are not properly and continually calibrated. In addition, they are heavy and expensive. In a school setting, depending on the level of detection, you would need a minimum of 3-4 people per machine. For proper use, you should have one person to check bags, another to focus on the machine itself and the third to use a hand wand to check any individual who set off the machine.

Try to imagine a school of 1,000 students coming in for the day. At best that detection station of three may be able to get 250 students through in an hour. A school of 1,000 would require four metal detectors and personnel to run each station. This would require a large budget. Would teachers run the stations? Would their contract or union allow that role?

Are you going to do a cursory check of each backpack, meaning you don't really search the entire bag, just feel for a weapon? What about metal belt buckles, buttons, rings, bracelets, etc? So, you lower the settings of the machine. Does that mean that now a partially plastic gun like a Glock can sneak through?

Metal detectors look good and might deter a shooter, but a dedicated shooter who is a student or former student can figure out how to get a gun into that school. There are many ways around a metal detector—throwing a backpack over the fence to be picked up later, passing it through a window or open door or bringing it in after school and hiding it somewhere to be used later.

Metal detectors are an expensive waste. The funds would be better used for better technology, more secure classroom doors and locks, front office lobby partitions and teacher training.

Smartphone Safety Apps

Many companies contacted me during my time with the school system, soliciting their various safety technologies. Some had very good ideas and a good track record with other school systems. Others were scams. My feeling on safety technology was that it had to be almost 100 percent guaranteed to work. If it were to fail, you just had to have a plan B.

One company had a good track record with an app that everyone could use and an indoor/outdoor camera system with zoom capabilities and swivel movement during a live event. There are also tech companies with expensive add-ons, such as heat signatures, weapons detection, microphones that can pick up conversations throughout the school and automatic lockdown of all doors.

One company wanted to utilize one of our high

schools for a test of the system they were promoting. It worked well in a practice setting and in a small meeting demo. However, the day we tried the app with our principal and assistant principal, it worked only on WIFI, which was intermittent within the school.

The app had some extremely valuable features. It had automatic alert to the police and fire departments. It had the capability of communication between the principals and teachers, documentation of the school safety plan, first aid procedures, contact lists and an area to list your students in attendance.

On the other hand, there were some issues. The app needed to be downloaded by every employee. Some might not want this app on their personal phones. Many would question privacy of the app, whether it collects personal information and location. This leads to a possible need to purchase staff business phones, an additional expense. Administrators must take all these issues into account before considering this type of technology.

The WIFI issue got resolved and within a month the high school had a real incident in which the app was put to the test. A student reported that he had seen someone in the boy's restroom with a gun. It took some time before the student reported it, so the school went into lockdown. The search for the gunman began.

Newer Technologies

With help from the SRO and local police, each classroom needed to be searched. During this real time event the app worked intermittently. Some teachers got the message through—most did not. The app went down in some locations or froze. After almost two hours of searching for this student, it was found out the entire incident was fake. There was no gun. However, it was a good test of this phone app.

My point is that we can't depend on technology alone. It can go down at the worst possible time. There must be a simple backup plan. Having the school safety plan checklist card that I described earlier can be a lifesaver. You can also take a picture of it and save on your phone. Technology is great when it works. But when it doesn't work—don't panic. Remember your training, keep yourself safe, then keep your students safe and stay quiet. Help is on the way.

CONCLUSION

I wrote this guide to give administrators, teachers, students and parents a resource to effectively prepare and train for a potential active shooter incident. To be effective, it is imperative that training and drills are done in the correct way, in order to impart mental memory so that reactions are more likely to become automatic. There is a misconception that successful methods of protection are expensive. However, there are many relatively affordable methods to protect your school from an intruder.

I wanted to focus exclusively on active shooter preparation and mitigation, because I am very passionate about the subject. I want to protect every child from becoming a victim of this type of tragedy. I have run into many scenarios while observing our school drills. I can't guarantee that I know the best way to handle each and every one; however, we must do our best to prepare because, sadly, there will always be another school shooting.

The purpose of this book is to help school administration make the best available choices to make their schools safe and give their staff the confidence in every situation in order to save lives. I strongly advise to have lockdown be the first option.

Ten affordable ways to keep your school safe from an active shooter assault:

1. Have one entrance into the school once the school day begins.
2. Lock all exterior doors other than the main entrance during school hours.
3. Lock all classroom doors and barricade them in the event a shooter tries to gain access.
4. Set up office lobbies so that visitors enter the office area and then are buzzed into the school once approved.
5. All office lobbies should have double-paned glass partitions to prevent an individual from jumping the counter or reaching over to grab office staff.
6. Middle and high school students should be encouraged to get involved in the safety of their school through a student safety council.

7. Check throughout the day that exterior doors are not wedged open with objects.
8. Staff should have a backup person assigned for emergency duties in case they are absent.
9. Keys should be available to the police either through the HPO or principal.
10. Train and drill correctly at a minimum of once per month.

One of the best examples of the importance of repetitive drilling and training for emergencies was during the 9/11 tragedy.

Rick Rescorla, a Vietnam veteran and head of security for Morgan Stanley Investments at the World Trade Center (WTC) building 2, required his staff to train repeatedly for fire drills. His drills took on added meaning after the 1993 bombing of the WTC. He would drill at any time and made sure every employee would walk down the 40 flights of stairs, no matter their title at the agency.

Employees would roll their eyes every time Rick ran a fire drill. Brokers had to leave their desks where high value money deals were occurring. Rick didn't care and made them do the drills.

Rick knew it was time when 9/11 occurred and building 1 was hit. Those drills were now becoming a reality. He took charge of getting thousands of Morgan Stanley employees safely out of that building. He then went back into building 2 but never made it out as the building collapsed. These heroic efforts were a direct result of his insistence on drilling at any time, unannounced, and making sure everyone followed and knew the protocols of getting out. His proven actions are a testament to repetitive drilling and acting the right way through habit and training.[1]

I have included a basic School Emergency plan which can be downloaded. It can be used for any level of school. Please scan the code below for a copy of my School Emergency Plan and General Procedures.

https://files.constantcontact.com/42ea7ecc001/
3b943ab8-9236-440f-85a4-c811d61c1bb9.pdf

The two photos on the next page are of an Elementary school lobby area. Double pane glass covers the front desk. The only door into the school has a key card access and the ability to be buzzed in by staff.

---

1 Ripley, Amanda. *The Unthinkable,* New York, N.Y. Three Rivers Press, 2008.

Conclusion

Secure lobby area with key card access

Secure lobby area with double pane glass

The link below contains a template of credit card size quick reference emergency cards that you can download and then have the cards laminated. These cards are invaluable for teachers as they can be attached to their ID passes or copier lanyards. They also can be photographed and available on your cell phones for quick references in an emergency.

https://files.constantcontact.com/42ea7ecc001/
0370cb8e-752a-49a0-904b-23134bf97a05.pdf

ABOUT THE AUTHOR
DAN DLUZNESKI

- Retired Lieutenant, U.S. Secret Service
- Former Coordinator, Emergency Management, Safety and Security, Pinellas County Schools

Growing up on a cattle farm in Connecticut, I developed a love of animals and I always had a desire to help others. I started my education at Southern Illinois University, majoring in Criminal Justice. After working in a variety of jobs, I decided to apply to the Uniformed Division of the United States Secret Service.

Career Highlights — Secret Service

- Over 24 years with the United States Secret Service
- Canine bomb detection unit, working with my dog Korak protecting the President, Vice President and their families
- Certified as a crime scene search technician

- Public Affairs Spokesperson
- Special Operations Officer, White House Historical tours

CAREER HIGHLIGHTS—PINELLAS COUNTY SCHOOLS

- CPTED certification
- Fire Inspector I, State of Florida
- Observed, supervised and coordinated over one hundred active shooter school drills.
- Standardized school emergency plans and procedures for active shooter drills

After my tenure in the Secret Service in 2013, I began working for the Pinellas County school system as the Coordinator of Emergency Management, Safety and Security. For 4 years, I was solely in charge of our entire county, which included over 140 schools and 104,000 students. I made certain that each school had an emergency plan, ran the proper drills and maintained their physical security barriers. I personally attended PTA, SAC and monthly teacher safety briefings, and produced training PowerPoints for principals and administrators to standardize the county drills and procedures. Attending national seminars and trainings, active shooter scenarios and certification through CPTED (crime prevention

About the Author

through environmental design) kept me up to date on all aspects of school safety. I am also a Fire Inspector I for the state of Florida.

My personal mission is to educate people within organizations about what to do in an emergency, such as an active shooter, fire or bomb threat. My background and experience is an invaluable tool to train people and help increase their confidence in responding to a threat. It is always better to be proactive and prepared for any situation.

Made in United States
North Haven, CT
15 February 2023